Happy Birthday,
Dear Anna,
Happy Birthday
To You!
August 29, 2001

Thought you might
enjoy a few small chunks
of Maine to have handy near
you in Indiana!

MAINE

MAINE

The Spirit of America

Text by Edgar Allen Beem

Harry N. Abrams, Inc., Publishers

NEW YORK

This series was originated by Walking Stick Press, San Francisco
Series Designer: Linda Herman; Series Editor: Diana Landau

For Harry N. Abrams, Inc.:
    Project Manager: Ruth A. Peltason
    Editor: Nicole Columbus
    Designer: Ana Rogers

Photo research:
    Laurie Platt Winfrey, Leslie Van Lindt, Van Bucher
    Carousel Research, Inc.

Page 1: *Photo Richard T. Nowitz/Corbis*
Page 2: Mount Katahdin, Baxter State Park. *Photo Kevin Shields*

Library of Congress Cataloguing-in-Publication Data
Beem, Edgar Allen, 1949–
    Maine : the spirit of America / text by Edgar Allen Beem.
    p.   cm.
    ISBN 0–8109–5570–9
    1. Maine—Miscellanea.   2. Maine—Civilization.   3. Maine—Civilization
    —Pictorial works.   4. Arts, American—Maine.   I. Title.   II. Series
F19.B43   2000
974.1—dc21   99–55231

Harry N. Abrams, Inc.
100 Fifth Avenue
New York, N.Y. 10011
www.abramsbooks.com

Carved and painted rustic hallstand, Sherman Station, Maine. c. 1870. *Photo Christie's Images*

CONTENTS

*"And they will love the land,
and the land will give back strength."*

Maine Civil War hero Joshua Chamberlain, Maine: Her Place in History, 1877

Maine is the end of the road. It is the easternmost state, the first place the sun shines every day in America. It is New England's big backyard. The legend on Maine license plates—decorated with lobsters, loons, and chickadees—reads "Vacationland," and, as the East Coast metropolis spreads inexorably north from Washington to New York and Boston, tourists flock to Maine for an experience of authenticity that's hard to find in more urban states.

The state markets itself for tourism and economic development with the slogan "Maine, The Way Life Should Be." This prescriptive phrase means to suggest a place where nature still exists in its relatively unspoiled state, where most people still live in small towns, where the pace of life is slow and thoughtful, attuned to the seasons and the elements. Portland, Maine's largest city, has a population of just 68,000. There is nowhere in the state that a resident cannot hunt, fish, swim, canoe, kayak, hike, or sail within a half hour of home.

Reveling in nature has a long tradition in Maine. When philosopher-naturalist Henry David Thoreau climbed mile-high Mount Katahdin in 1846,

The Artist Sketching at Mount Desert, Maine by Sanford Robinson Gifford, 1864–65. *Collection Joann and Julian Ganz*

his transcendentalist soul leaped for joy at the trackless wilderness spread out before him. "Think of our life in nature," Thoreau enthused in *The Maine Woods,* "daily to be shown matter, to come in contact with it,—rocks, trees, wind on our cheeks! the *solid* earth! the *actual* world!" In the wilds of Maine, Thoreau found "a specimen of what God saw fit to make this world."

Maine is an elemental place. It is the most heavily forested of the lower 48 states, and it has the longest coastline. The climate is harsh and unforgiving. Winter is long, dark, and cold. Spring is mud season. Summer is brief, and fall glorious. The character of the people who live here—just 1.2 million in an area as large as all the rest of New England—is molded by the same forces that shaped the landscape. Mainers tend to be hardy, independent, and down to earth; common sense is the coin of the realm.

The state's political leaders—from Margaret Chase Smith and Edmund Muskie to George Mitchell and William Cohen—typically are people of moderation and conscience. The writers Maine has nurtured—from poets Henry Wadsworth Longfellow and Edwin Arlington Robinson to essayist E. B. White

Seated Bear by Bernard Langlais, n.d.
Ogunquit Museum of American Art, Me.

and novelist Stephen King—have tended to possess the common touch. And the visual artists who have flourished here— from Winslow Homer and Marsden Hartley to Andrew Wyeth and Neil Welliver—have generally been ornery realists.

In the Pine Tree State, the environment *is* the economy. More than 10 million visitors a year flock to the state's lakes, rivers, forests, mountains, coast, and islands. The things Mainers produce are also tied closely to the land and sea. Two of the state's largest employers are shipyards: Bath Iron Works and Portsmouth–Kittery Naval Shipyard. Dozens of small boatyards turn out everything from canoes and kayaks to rowing shells, dories, sloops, and fishing boats.

Thousands still make their livings hauling logs out of the woods and lobsters out of the sea, digging clams and worms at the shore, trapping eels in the rivers, picking potatoes in the rolling fields of Aroostook County. Ten major paper companies—the

Culminating Lace of the Ferry Master's Garden by Jill Hoy, 1991. Collection of Henry and Jody McCorcles

state's largest industry—turn wood pulp of the North Woods into everything from tissue and newsprint to fine coated papers for books and magazines.

Maine was part of Massachusetts until 1820 and is still grudgingly dependent on the urban economy to the south, but Mainers prize self-reliance and identify strongly with their state. Nativity is a virtue: a person can live in Maine for 50 years and still be considered "from away." On certain islands off the coast, folks still speak with accents that Shakespeare would recognize. Even being born here may not count for much if your parents weren't—as an old downeast saying goes, "Just because a cat has kittens in the oven doesn't make them biscuits."

Still, a fair amount of chauvinism is well-grounded. Maine is a state with a true sense of place and countless places still worth preserving. 🌲

MAINE

"Pine Tree State"
23rd State

Date of Statehood
MARCH 15, 1820

Capital
AUGUSTA

Bird
CHICKADEE

Flower
PINE CONE AND TASSEL

Tree
WHITE PINE

Animal
MOOSE

Cat
MAINE COON CAT

Fish
LANDLOCKED SALMON

Gemstone
TOURMALINE

"Ðirigo" (I lead)

State motto

Maine is the Pine Tree State, a heavily forested land where agents of the British crown came in the 18th century to cut tall, straight king's pines for ships' masts. No hothouse blooms or fragile wildflowers for rugged Maine, whose state "flower" is the white pine cone and tassel.

Chickadee and pine cone

The state bird is the little black-capped chickadee, a hardy year-round resident of the North Woods. Indeed, Maine's symbols all tend toward the common, tenacious, and resourceful. On the state seal a farmer and a mariner flank a lone pine before which rests a moose, lord of the Maine forest. Above rises the North Star and the state's motto, *Dirigo,* meaning "I lead." Maine leads the nation in, among other things, the catch of lobsters—yet another symbol of this cold, coastal state. 🌲

Purr-fect Pets

Everything in Maine has origins in the woods or the water, and the popular Maine Coon Cat is no exception. The only natural breed of domestic American cat, it is thought to have sprung from the interbreeding of ships' cats with bobcats (which it resembles) and lynx. Coon Cats were originally kept as mousers, but starting in the 1860s farmers exhibited their favorite felines at agricultural fairs, earning the breed a reputation as America's first show cats.

Maine Coon Cat, a silver tabby. *Photo J-L Klein and M-L Hubert/ Okapia/Photo Researchers. Top:* The Maine state seal, painted on silk by E. W. Parkhurst, mid-19th century. *Maine State Museum, Augusta. Left:* Pitch pines stand fast against the sea breezes in Acadia National Park. *Photo Michael Gadomski, Photo Researchers*

Fried Clams in Batter

Elsewhere along the East Coast, soft-shell clams are fried in crumbs, but real Mainers prefer fritterlike fried clams coated in batter. Herewith a recipe from the annual Yarmouth Clam Festival:

1 pint shucked clams, rinsed and drained
Fat for deep frying, heated to 375 degrees

Batter
1 egg
½ cup milk
¼ teaspoon salt
1 tablespoon melted butter
½ cup sifted flour

Separate egg. Mix yolk with milk, salt, and butter, then stir in flour. Beat egg white until stiff, then fold in yolk mixture. Dip clams individually in batter, then fry until golden brown. Drain on absorbent paper.

Lobster Plate to Go

In 1986, at the behest of a group of Saco schoolchildren, Maine replaced its no-nonsense black-and-white vehicle license plates with one that featured a red lobster. Although *Homarus americanus* is universally associated with Maine, live lobsters are blue-black in color, and many Mainers took umbrage at sporting a cooked crustacean on their plates. After years of good-natured grousing, the lobster plates are now being phased out, replaced by ones featuring loons or chickadees.

The Sole of Maine

A down-to-earth symbol for a cold, damp state is the Maine Hunting Shoe, a.k.a. the Bean Boot. Designed by Leon Leonwood Bean and first sold in Freeport in 1912, the Bean Boot—rubber bottoms stitched to leather uppers—is the ideal footwear for a landscape of woods, streams, and bogs. L. L. Bean created the boot for hunting, but these days it's as apt to turn up on Manhattan streets as on North Woods trails.

Much Ado About Moose

Although there are nearly 10 times as many white-tail deer (292,000) and roughly the same number of black bears (23,000) in the Maine woods as there are moose (30,000), the lumbering lord of the forest gets the nod as official state animal. Since 1982 the state has permitted as many as 2,000 moose a year to be killed by hunters. Critics of the fall moose hunt have argued that the only thing sporting about shooting such a large, lethargic animal is getting it to fall close enough to a road so hunters don't have to haul a 1,500-pound carcass out of the woods. Still, with car–moose accidents on the rise, Maine's moose hunt seems more likely to expand than be banned.

Moose, Baxter State Park. *PhotoFarrell Grehan/Photo Researchers*

Some Downeast Lingo

Ayuh Yes. Can be drawn out into *aaay-yuh* or clipped and swallowed: *'yuh*

Blow down Lumbering term for limbs and trees blown down by the wind. Other woods words include *dri-ki* (freshwater driftwood, remnants of logging), *widow maker* (a broken limb or tree that might yet fall on a logger), and *deadfall* (a mass of brush and limbs, or a dead tree fallen on its own).

Dear (*DEE-ah*) Old-timers and a few hard-core downeasters use *dear* dispassionately to address anyone, regardless of age or gender.

Downeast A sailing term; literally, the direction of the prevailing wind from Boston to Nova Scotia. Sometimes used to designate Maine generally; specifically denotes the Maine coast above Mount Desert Island

Finestkind The best, a term of appreciation

From away Anyone not a Maine native

Haulin' Tending lobster traps

Jeezly All-purpose adjective or adverb apparently unrelated to Jesus. "It's jeezly cold out there, ain't it, Bub?"

Junk The Maine way to say "chunk"

Some Universal adjective meaning "very," as in "Ain't she some pretty!"

Thick o' fog When the fog's so thick he can't go haulin', a lobsterman's apt to say something like, "Ayuh, it's thick o' junk o' fog out there."

Wicked good Extremely good, another term of appreciation

A.D. **1000–1010** Norsemen, including Leif Erikson, explore the coast of Maine.

1497–99 John and Sebastian Cabot explore coast of Maine, establishing English claims.

1524 Giovanni da Verrazano explores coast for the French.

1603 Martin Pring maps the coast from the Piscataqua to the Penobscot River.

1606 James I grants rights to southern Maine to the Plymouth Company.

1607–8 Popham Colony settled and abandoned.

1622 Sir Fernando Gorges and John Mason granted all lands between the Merrimac River and Kennebec River, establishing Province of Maine—first official use of "Maine."

1626–29 English trading posts established at Pentagoet (Castine), Cushnoc (Augusta), Richmond, and Machias.

1652 Province of Maine comes under jurisdiction of Massachusetts Bay Colony.

1675–1755 French and Indian Wars. Many settlements destroyed by Indian and French attacks, but English prevail.

1742 Population estimated at 12,000.

1755 Acadians dispersed throughout American colonies.

1770 Population estimated at 31,000.

1775 Benedict Arnold leads ill-fated expedition through Maine to Quebec. British burn Falmouth (Portland). British vessel *Margaretta* captured at Machias in first naval battle of the American Revolution.

1788 Slavery abolished in Maine.

1790 George Washington orders Portland Head Light built. Population estimated at 96,500.

1794 Bowdoin College, Maine's first college, established in Brunswick.

1807 Poet Henry Wadsworth Longfellow born in Portland.

1810 Population: 228,705.

1812 British attack Maine, occupy coast during War of 1812.

1820 Maine separates from Massachusetts, becomes a state under Missouri Compromise. Population: 298,335.

1838 Aroostook War, a bloodless boundary dispute between Maine and New Brunswick; only American "war" declared by a state against a foreign nation.

1851 The Maine Law, the nation's first strong prohibition act, outlaws the manufacture or sale of liquor in Maine.

1861–65 72,945 Maine men fight for the Union in the Civil War.

1863 Gen. Joshua Chamberlain and the 20th Maine Regiment valiantly defend Little Round Top during Battle of Gettysburg.

1866 Joshua Chamberlain becomes governor. Some 2,000 buildings burn during Great

Portland Fire, touched off by Fourth of July fireworks.

1869 Poet Edward Arlington Robinson born in Lewiston.

1870 Population: 626,915.

1877 Marsden Hartley born in Lewiston.

1882 Portland Museum of Art founded.

1884 Bath Iron Works (shipyard), Maine's largest employer, founded. Former Maine Sen. James G. Blaine runs for president.

1892 Poet Edna St. Vincent Millay born in Rockland.

1894 Walker Art Building by Charles McKim dedicated at Bowdoin College.

1898 Battleship *Maine* blown up in Havana Harbor. "Remember the *Maine*" becomes battle cry of the Spanish-American War.

1919 Lafayette National Park (Acadia National Park after 1928) established by Congress on Mount Desert Island.

1931 Ex-Governor Percival Baxter gives Mt. Katahdin State Park to state.

1934 Maine Law repealed, ending Prohibition.

1940 Population: 847,226.

1941 South Portland Shipyard established. Some 30,000 Mainers build 266 ships during World War II.

1947 Skowhegan School of Painting and Sculpture opens.

1947 Bar Harbor, summer watering hole of the rich, destroyed by fire. Novelist Stephen King born in Portland.

1948 Margaret Chase Smith is the first woman elected to the U.S. Senate.

1950 Sen. Smith's "Declaration of Conscience Speech" spells the beginning of the end of Sen. Joseph McCarthy's communist witch hunt.

1951 Haystack Mountain School of Crafts opens.

1952 Ogunquit Museum of Art opens.

1959 Colby College Museum of Art founded.

1963 Landmark show "Maine and Its Role in American Art" at Colby College documents state's artistic heritage.

1975 Last river drive in Maine.

1979 Sen. Edmund Muskie named secretary of state.

1980 Indian Land Claims Settlement gives Passaquoddy, Penobscot, and Maleseet tribes $81.5 million for their ancestral lands.

1986 Maine voters approve $35 million fund for purchasing wildlands for public use.

1990 Population: 1,227,928.

1998 Sen. William Cohen, named secretary of defense by President Clinton. Farnsworth Center for the Wyeth Family in Maine opens in Rockland.

Wreck of the D. T. Sheridan by Rockwell Kent, c. 1949–53. The coast of Maine is as treacherous as it is beautiful. Kent incorporated the rusted hull of a tugboat that went aground on Monhegan Island in 1948 as an element of this otherwise peaceful composition. *Portland Museum of Art, Me.*

> *"Nature was here something savage and awful, though beautiful."*
>
> Henry David Thoreau, The Maine Woods, *1864*

Maine is a landscape defined and determined by water. Some 25,000 years ago a great glacier spread south over the entire state and then receded 7,000 years later. Left in its wake was a raw, scoured land drained by 5,000 rivers and streams, sparkling with 6,000 lakes and ponds, and blessed offshore with 4,600 saltwater islands. As the glacier melted and retreated, it drowned the coast, creating a chaos of islands, bays, peninsulas, and inlets. Although the coast of Maine is only 228 miles long as the crow flies, if the shoreline were straightened out it would stretch to 3,500 miles (5,500, if you add the island shorelines).

Maine's northern border with Canada is formed by the St. John River, its southern border with New Hampshire by the Piscataqua. In between, the Saco, Androscoggin, Kennebec, and Penobscot rivers flow down out of the western mountains through the most heavily forested landscape in the United States. 🌲

Acadian barns, Aroostook County. "The County" is Maine's chief agricultural region, a landscape of rolling potato fields and northern farms. *Photo Brian Vanden Brink*

Drift in Beach by Thomas Crotty, 1995. Thomas Crotty started Frost Gully Gallery, Maine's oldest contemporary art gallery, in 1966. *Thomas Crotty/Private collection*

Along Shore

The Maine coast has three distinct personalities. Sand beaches sweep up from Massachusetts as far as Cape Elizabeth, making York County a mecca for beach lovers. The mid-coast, from Portland to Mount Desert Island, is where the fabled "rock-bound coast of Maine" begins, in a tatter of peninsulas and bays, inlets and estuaries, islands and ledges. Down East, from Mount Desert to Lubec, the coast becomes a dramatic landscape of steep cliffs, bold headlands, and wild blueberry barrens. Known locally as "the bold coast," here the shore rock stands as a bulwark against some of the highest tides in the world, as the waters of the Gulf of Maine swirl counterclockwise into the Bay of Fundy.

Mount Desert Island

Mount Desert Island, home of Bar Harbor and Acadia National Park, is the only place on the eastern seaboard where mountains fall directly into the sea. The island's spectacular scenery has been attracting visitors since the dawn of tourism in the 1870s. Today more than 3 million visitors a year seek out Acadia National Park for its unparalleled system of hiking trails and carriage roads, its mountaintop ocean vistas and unique natural wonders such as Thunder Hole, Sand Beach, and Somes Sound—the only fjord on the East Coast. Cadillac Mountain is the first place in America to see the sun each day, so many visitors drive to the summit at dawn to be first in the nation to greet the new day.

Above: Dorothy Stanley Emmons on rocks at Ogunquit Pond by Chansonetta Stanley Emmons, c. 1910. Emmons, a pioneering Maine photographer, captured romantic images of rural life during the Age of Innocence. *Culver Pictures. Right:* Shoreline near Acadia National Park. *Photo Kevin Shields*

The Swimmer by Yasuo Kuniyoshi, c. 1924. Kuniyoshi summered at the Ogunquit art colony and brought a Modernist aesthetic to bear on the coastal Maine landscape. *Columbus Museum of Art, Ohio. © Estate of Yasuo Kuniyoshi/Licensed by VAGA, New York, N.Y.*

The Maine coast is strung with a garland of islands, ranging from treeless sea-bird rookeries to majestic Mount Desert. Only about a dozen of Maine's myriad islands are inhabited year round, but storied isles such as Monhegan, Matinicus, Islesboro, North Haven, Vinalhaven, Swan's Island, and Isle Au Haut are Maine in microcosm—rocky shores, thick spruce woods, sparse population, fishing villages, artists' colonies, summer estates, and wild weather. The Maine Island Trail system maps a 325-mile waterway that gives sea kayakers and sailors access to an offshore paradise of 80 private and public islands. ♣

"OUR LIVES THERE, MY BROTHERS' AND SISTER'S AND MINE, WERE from the first determined by the sea. High tide was the time to swim; and low tide the time to explore the shore. . . . We gathered shells along the high-tide wrack: powder blue and purple mussels in all sizes that nested together in compact families; pale green sea urchins washed clean of their spines; and the perfectly preserved, brilliant orange carapaces shed by the small, brown-green crabs that live in the rock weed of the littoral zone."

Eliot Porter, Summer Island: Penobscot Country, *1966*

Painting the Coast of Maine by Janice Kasper, 1999. Maine's pictur-esque, rock-bound coast is a magnet for artists and tourists alike. Private collection. Photo Peggy McKenna

Fall view of Mount Katahdin, Baxter State Park. *Photo Kevin Shields*
Below: River otters (*Lutra canadensis*) were once fairly abundant in Maine's waterways but are now among the rarer denizens of the northern forest. *Photo Stephen J. Krasemann/ Photo Researchers*

The Rivers and the County

The great rivers of the Gulf of Maine watershed gave explorers and settlers their first access to Maine's interior fastness. Paper and textile mills sprang up along the Saco, Androscoggin, Penobscot, and Kennebec to take advantage of the abundant woods and water power. River drives floated logs out of the North Woods until 1975. Today, after two decades of stringent environmental laws, dams are coming down and whitewater rafting, canoeing, and fishing are replacing industry along the rivers.

The mighty St. John River along Maine's northern border defines Aroostook County, Maine's prime agricultural region. Known simply as "the County,"

Aroostook is a landscape of rolling potato fields roughly the size of Connecticut and Rhode Island combined. In 1999, Maine potato growers planted 67,000 acres, but only about 25 percent of the harvest now goes to market fresh. Another 25 percent is planted in seed potato, but most of the spuds are big Russet Burbanks, used to make french fries, and proprietary strains of small, waxy potatoes that become Frito-Lay chips. Proximity to Canada gives the County its distinctive Acadian heritage and Franco-American population.

Mount Katahdin, Maine by Marsden Hartley, 1939–40. Hartley considered himself *the* painter of Maine, and the paintings he made during a brief trip to Katahdin in the fall of 1939 rank among his masterpieces. *The Metropolitan Museum of Art, New York*

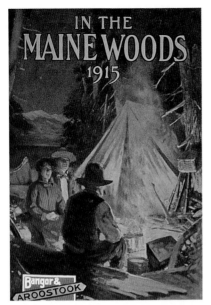

The Bangor & Aroos-
took Railroad once
promoted Maine's
North Woods for hunt-
ing, fishing, and tourism
in colorful brochures.
Maine Historical Society

Taking to the Woods

Maine's North Woods are a "transition
forest" of coniferous and deciduous
woodlands bristling with spruce, pine,
and fir and alive with deer, bear and
moose, blackflies, and loggers. Maine is
the nation's most heavily forested state,
with close to 90 percent of the land cov-
ered in trees. Vast tracts of the North
Woods are owned by major paper companies and administered by the Land
Use Regulation Commission as unorga-
nized territories. Divided into square
"townships," the woods have been cut
at different rates over the years, so that
the political boundaries of this checker-
board landscape are now visible from
satellites in space.

Efforts to preserve Maine's north
country have resulted in the 92-mile-long Allagash Wilderness
Waterway and 200,000-acre Baxter State Park, purchased by former Governor Percival Baxter and given to the state in 1931. At
the center of this natural splendor stands mile-high Mount
Katahdin, the Maine landscape's crown jewel.

"MONUMENTS DECAY, BUILDINGS CRUMBLE AND WEALTH VANISHES,
but Katahdin in its massive grandeur will forever remain the
mountain of the people of Maine."

Former Governor Percival Baxter, 1941

Sand Pool by Neil Welliver, 1998. One of America's foremost landscape painters, Welliver tends to focus on woodland interiors in which he methodically sorts out the visual complexity of nature. *Private collection. Courtesy Tibor de Nagy Gallery, New York*

A pair of Micmac beaded hide moccasins. *Photo Christie's Images. Opposite top:* Squanto was a member of the Pawtuxet tribe. *Culver Pictures. Opposite bottom:* Canoes, such as this one used by the Penobscot tribe, were the perfect mode of transportation along the Maine coast and upriver into the forest interior. *Photo David Brownell*

People of the Dawn

The native and natural people of Maine numbered perhaps 20,000 before contact with European explorers. Paleo-Indians settled on the tundra left in the wake of glaciers that receded some 11,000 years ago. A distinctive group of these early natives inhabited the region between 5,000 and 3,800 years ago, building burial mounds on North Haven and Vinalhaven and in Brooklin and Blue Hill. Archaeologists branded them the "Red Paint People" after the bright red ochre (hematite powder) discovered in the mounds.

The modern-day Penobscot, Passamaquoddy, Micmac, and Maliseet tribes of Maine are all Wabanakis— "People of the Dawn." Their ancestors were woodland Indians who spoke Algonquian and existed on caribou, deer, beaver, fish, and clams. An estimated 75 percent of the Wabanaki (or Abenaki) people perished between 1616 and 1619 as a result of the Great Dying, a plague of virulent diseases brought ashore by European explorers. In 1980 the U.S. government made reparations for taking the ancestral lands of Maine's native people by settling their land claims suit for $81.5 million. 🌲

We sing on the road of the spirits;
The road of the great spirit.
Among us are three hunters
Who follow the bear,
There never was a time
When they were not hunting.
We look upon the mountains
This is a song of the mountains.

Passamaquoddy legend, recorded in 1921

A Morning View of Blue Hill Village by Jonathan Fisher, 1824. Parson Fisher painted some of the earliest Maine landscapes. Just four years after statehood, his vision of Blue Hill captures civilization taking hold in the wilds of Maine. *Farnsworth Art Museum, Rockland, Me. Photo Melville D. McLean Below:* Italian navigator Giovanni da Verrazano (1485–1528) explored the coast of Maine for France in 1524. *Corbis*

Exploring "The Main"

There are stories of Viking sailors and Celtic fishermen plying the wild coast of Maine as early as the 10th century, but it wasn't until the dawn of the 16th century, the Age of Discovery, that the first European visits to Maine shores were documented. In 1497–99, John and Sebastian Cabot made a number of landings on the North Atlantic coast, establishing an English claim to the region. Then, in 1524, Italian explorer Giovanni da Verrazano, sailing for France, entered Casco Bay and made a French claim, setting the stage for an English–French rivalry that would not be settled for 200 years. In 1604 the French attempted to found a colony on St. Croix Island, near present-day Machias, and the English tried to plant what is known as

the Popham Colony near present-day Phippsburg in 1607, but neither settlement survived Maine's harsh winters. European settlements and trading posts began to pop up in the wilderness in the 1620s, but by 1632, when the French raided the English settlement at Pentagoet, the invading white men were already at each other's throats.

Samuel de Champlain (1567–1635) explored and mapped the coast of Maine for France in 1604. Champlain named Mount Desert Island and helped establish the French claim to the region, setting the stage for a century of territorial wars: the French and their Indian allies fighting the English. *Corbis-Bettmann*

"THE TWELFTH DAY OF JULY . . . I TOOK BOAT FOR THE EASTERN PARTS of the Countrie, and arrived at Black point in the province of Main, which is 150 miles from Boston. . . . The Countrey all along as I sailed, being no other than a meer Wilderness, here and there by the Sea-side a few scattered plantations, with as few houses."

John Josselyn, 1638. Josselyn's classic Two Voyages to New-England, *published in 1674, is rich in observations of the region's geography and natural history.*

War on the Frontier

The French and Indian Wars began with King Philip's War in 1675 and did not end until peace was brokered at Maine's Fort Pownall in 1762. Throughout this time, attempts to settle Maine's wild frontier were thwarted not only by the hostile climate but by constant warring between the English

on the one side and the French and Indians on the other. The outcome left the English in control of New England and the French confined to Canada. In 1755 the British expelled 10,000 French-speaking Acadians from Nova Scotia, inspiring Maine poet Henry Wadsworth Longfellow's epic poem "Evangeline."

THE TOWN of FALMOUTH, *Burnt by Captain* MOET, O

Many Acadians eventually settled in the St. John River Valley, where their descendants live to this day.

Almost as soon as the French and English ceased fighting, American colonists began to resist British rule. In the first naval battle of the Revolutionary War (June 1775), Machias residents captured the HMS *Margaretta*. In October, the British retaliated by burning Falmouth (present-day Portland) to the ground and sinking the local merchant fleet. That fall, Colonel Benedict Arnold marched 1,100 men through the wilds of Maine in an ill-fated attempt to capture Quebec and roust the British. Close to half of Arnold's men perished along the way.

Massacre of York & Wells, Maine by Royal Lewando. This 20th-century mural depicts a 1692 Indian attack on the British settlement at York during the French and Indian Wars. *Private collection*

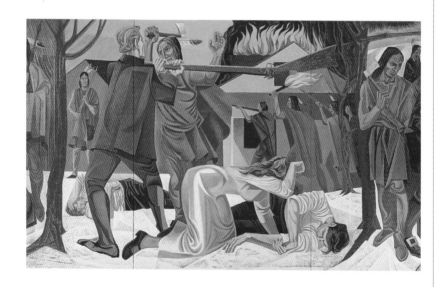

Maine joined the newly independent United States in 1820 as a result of the Missouri Compromise. To balance slave states and free states, Missouri was admitted to the Union as a slave state and Maine, which had abolished slavery in 1788, as a free state. When the issue of slavery came to a head with the Civil War, Mainers played a pivotal role. Indeed, it might be said that one Maine resident started the Civil War and another ended it.

135,000 SETS, 270,000 VOLUMES SOLD.

UNCLE TOM'S CABIN

FOR SALE HERE.

AN EDITION FOR THE MILLION, COMPLETE IN 1 Vol, PRICE 37 1-2 CENTS.
" " IN GERMAN, IN 1 Vol, PRICE 50 CENTS.
" " IN 2 Vols, CLOTH, 6 PLATES, PRICE $1.50.
SUPERB ILLUSTRATED EDITION, IN 1 Vol, WITH 153 ENGRAVINGS,
PRICES FROM $2.50 TO $5.00.

The Greatest Book of the Age.

Harriet Beecher Stowe wrote *Uncle Tom's Cabin* while living in Brunswick. Abraham Lincoln credited Stowe's book with helping to spark the Civil War. *Courtesy New-York Historical Society*

Harriet Beecher Stowe wrote her anti-slavery novel Uncle Tom's Cabin while living in Brunswick. Abraham Lincoln credited Stowe with being "the little lady who wrote the book that started this great war." Stowe's Brunswick neighbor Joshua Chamberlain, who taught at Bowdoin College along with Stowe's husband, commanded the valiant Twentieth Maine Regiment, which—outnumbered and nearly surrounded—nonetheless charged into Confederate ranks at Little Round Top to save the day and the Union at the Battle of Gettysburg. For his courage and valor, General Chamberlain, who would later become president of Bowdoin and governor of Maine, was chosen to accept the Confederate surrender at Appomattox. 🌲

"Bayonet! Forward!"

*Joshua Chamberlain, leading the charge of the 20th
Maine Regiment at the Battle of Little Round Top*

Colonel Joshua L. Chamberlain, 1863. Chamberlain was the
hero of the Battle of Little Round Top and later became
president of Bowdoin College and governor of Maine.
Pejepscot Historical Society

Maine's Historic Sites

**Abbe Museum of Stone Age
Antiquities**
Bar Harbor, 207-288-3519

Colonial Pemaquid Museum
Pemaquid, 207-677-2423

Fort Popham Historic Site
Popham, 207-389-1335

Joshua Chamberlain Museum
Brunswick, 207-729-6606

Maine State Museum
Augusta, 207-287-2301

**Montpelier (Gen. Henry Knox
Mansion)**
Thomaston, 207-354-8062

Wadsworth-Longfellow House
Portland, 207-879-0427

This 1861 snare drum is among the
Civil War artifacts in the collection of
the Maine State Museum. *Maine State
Museum, Augusta*

The Paper Plantation

Maine's 17 million acres of forestland are its greatest renewable resource. First harvested for the mast trade in colonial days, forests provided the raw material from which Maine homes and ships were built well into the

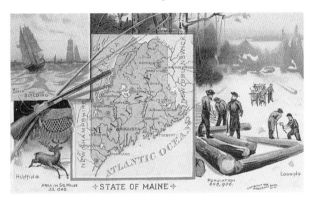

19th century. By 1906, moreover, there were 109 pulp and paper mills in Maine, making forest products the state's primary industry. Lumberjacks working with axes and bucksaws, oxen and draft horses worked all winter to fell trees, "twitch" them out of the woods, and yard them up for spring log drives, when great rafts of logs were floated downriver. River drivers, armed only with cleated boots and hooked poles called peaveys, rode and wrestled the floating logs downstream to the mills. Today's loggers

As this 1889 postcard makes abundantly clear, the Maine economy has long been based on the natural resources of its woods and waters.
Corbis-Bettmann

work the woods with a mechanical fleet of skidders, feller-bunchers, and whole tree chippers, supplying Maine's ten paper mills with fiber to make everything from newsprint and tissue to the finest coated papers. The river drives ended in 1975, and the woods are now ribboned with a network of paper-company roads over which huge logging trucks rumble from dawn to dusk. 🌲

Above: A truckload of pulp logs arrives at the Boise Cascade (now Mead Paper) mill in Rumford. *Photo Joe Sohm/Photo Researchers. Below:* The family farm was the mainstay of the Maine economy until the early 20th century. *Culver Pictures*

THERE UNDER THE BARK OF THAT SPRUCE THERE IS FURLED
A web that will carry the news of a world,
That clamors and crowds at the swaying red backs
Of the toilers of Maine, the rough men of the axe.

Holman Day, "The Chap That Swings the Axes," 1901

Every Maine lobsterman paints his buoys a different color in order to identify his own traps on the water; these are in Bass Harbor. *Photo Bruce Hayes/Photo Researchers. Below:* Though Burnham & Morrill in Portland is now best-known for baking and canning B&M brand beans, it once tinned Maine's native delicacy as Red Jacket Brand Lobster. *Maine State Archives*

Gone Haulin'

Lobsters are so plentiful along the Maine coast that they were once disdained—fed to servants and used as fertilizer. No more. Today, lobsters account for roughly half the value of Maine's $270-million-a-year commercial fishery, as some 7,000 lobstermen tend close to 2.6 million traps from Kittery to Calais. In the old days, lobstermen rowed dories from hand-

made wooden trap to trap and hand-hauled their catch aboard. Their modern counterparts put to sea in $100,000 boats, hauling wire-mesh traps out of the cold North Atlantic with hydraulic winches. Still, the sight of high-prowed lobster boats working the waters like bees collecting pollen is one of the most distinctive images of coastal Maine.

However picturesque, lobstering is hard work and highly regulated to sustain the resource. Only lobsters that measure from 3¼ inches to 5 inches from eye socket to the rear of the body shell are legal "keepers." Lobstermen tend to be fiercely territorial; trap wars sometimes break out when boats stray into waters traditionally fished by others. Blissfully ignorant of all this are most diners who frequent Maine's lobster pounds, where the delicacy is served "in the rough," steamed with melted butter, a shell cracker, and a bib.

"THERE'LL BE DAYS YOU THINK YOU'RE GOING to get rich, but you don't. And there'll be days you think you're going to starve, but you won't."

Seventh-generation lobsterman Maynard Brewer on the advice his father gave him when he started lobstering

Above: A sternman baits lobster traps in Quahog Bay while gulls wait for scraps. *Photo Jeff Greenberg/Photo Researchers. Left:* Atlantic salmon are raised up and down the coast of Maine in pens such as these in Eastport. *Photo Brian Vanden Brink*

Wooden boat building is still a fine art in Maine. Here, work progresses on the deck of the windjammer *Grace Bailey* during a complete rebuild. *Photo Kevin Shields*

Maine's shipbuilding tradition is almost 400 years old. The first ship built in the New World was the *Virginia,* a 30-ton pinnace made by the Popham colonists near Phippsburg in 1607. Since then, Maine shipbuilders have built everything from clipper ships and square-rigged downeasters to Liberty ships and destroyers. The heyday of sail in the 19th century was a boom time for Maine shipwrights. The trades in rum, grain, ice, and lime all required fast commercial vessels, and speed became even more important in the 1850s, after gold was discovered in

California. By 1880, close to 200,000 Mainers were employed in shipyards in 50 different towns along the coast.

During World War II, 30,000 shipbuilders worked round the clock in South Portland, building 266 ships in four years, or one Liberty ship every five days. Today, Bath Iron Works on the Kennebec River remains one of the state's largest employers. Maine shipbuilders build Aegis class destroyers for the U.S. Navy, and the Portsmouth Naval Shipyard in Kittery services submarines for the Navy. ⚓

Bath Iron Works, one of Maine's largest employers, builds destroyers for the U.S. Navy at its shipyard on the Kennebec River. *Photo Kevin Shields*

"THE HEART OF A SHIP COMES FROM PEOPLE LIKE THOSE IN BATH, whose brains and sweat have designed and built her. . . . That is one reason why so many officers and men like to serve on the powerful and rugged ships built by the Bath Iron Works."

Admiral Arleigh A. Burke, Chief of Naval Operations, 1956

Welcome to Vacationland

Tourism brings $4.8 billion a year to Maine and employs more than 100,000 residents, making it the state's second-largest industry after papermaking. And both depend on the same natural resources—woods and water. "Rusticators" first started coming to the Maine coast after the Civil War, lured out of the teeming southerly cities by the prospect of cool breezes, scenic ocean vistas, and simple country living. Summer colonies grew up in places like Bar Harbor, Dark Harbor, Camden, Prouts Neck, and Boothbay Harbor. Artists' colonies arose on Monhegan Island and in the beachfront community of Ogunquit. Old Orchard Beach became the Coney Island of Maine. In the days of steamers and trains, whole families came for the summer, but as automobiles and air travel brought Maine closer to the cities, Vacationland visits shortened from months to days.

The focus of summer tourism remains coastal Maine and the lakes, but the state is a four-season destination, attracting hunters and "leaf-peepers" in the fall, skiers and snowmobilers in the winter, and fishermen in the spring. The number-one tourist activity, however, is shopping. During the 1980s, Freeport, home of L. L. Bean, and Kittery, Maine's gateway city, became retail outlet boomtowns.

The Great Falls Balloon Festival is an annual event in Lewiston/Auburn. *Photo Alan J. LaVallee*

Vinalhaven by Thomas Crotty, 1996. Ferries run daily to many of Maine's island communities. *Private collection. Below:* Maine's western mountains provide some of the East's best ski terrain. *Photo David Brownell*

"THE LITTLE HOUSES OF THE ORIGINAL HALF FARMERS, HALF fishermen, who welcomed, or rather did not welcome, the first explorers, grew rapidly into little boarding-houses, then into big boarding-houses, then into hotels with registers. Then the hotels grew larger and larger, and the callings of the steamer more frequent, until the place became famous and crowded."

*Journalist Edward Lawrence Godkin,
describing the evolution of Bar Harbor, 1895*

Andrew Wyeth painted the German Lutheran Church in Waldoboro.
Photo Brian Vanden Brink

Maine's religious life is predominantly Christian, with some 220,000 Roman Catholics and a like number professing various Protestant faiths. The most distinctive denomination is the smallest: the United Society of Believers, popularly known as Shakers, has maintained a settlement at Sabbathday Lake in New Gloucester since 1783. Today the five members of that community are the only Shakers left in the world.

Mother Ann Lee brought the Shaker ideals of Christian love, celibacy, pacifism, equality, and communal sharing of work and possessions to America from England in 1774. By 1850, some 6,000 Shakers lived in 23 communities in 11 states. Their philosophy of simple living begat a design aesthetic seen in the elegantly functional furniture and tools for which Shakers are renowned. The little village at Sabbathday Lake maintains among its 13 spartan buildings a museum of Shaker history and crafts. The celibate Shakers have always depended on conversion for their continued existence, and in 1965, the community at Canterbury, New Hampshire—one of only two remaining Shaker societies—closed its membership, dooming itself to extinction. The Sabbathday Lake Shakers, however, remained open to new members and so struggle on into the 21st century. 🌲

Below left: **The last few Shakers on earth live at Sabbathday Lake in Maine.** *Photo Brian Vanden Brink. Below right:* **White steeples like the one atop East Machias Congregational Church punctuate the skylines of small-town Maine.** *Photo Brian Vanden Brink*

"Put your hands to work, and your hearts to God."

Shaker motto

Lighthouse at Two Lights by Edward Hopper, 1929. Hopper's evocations of the lonely sentinels of the Maine coast have never been improved upon. *The Metropolitan Museum of Art, N.Y.*

Sentinels of the Coast

Sixty-four active lighthouses stand watch along the Maine coast, from Whaleback Light at the entrance to the Piscataqua River to the bold red-and-white striped West Quoddy Light at Lubec, on the easternmost point in the continental U.S. These sentinels of the coast are still aids to navigation but also links to Maine's historic and artistic past. The oldest, Portland Head Light in Cape Elizabeth—

built in 1791 per order of President George Washington—is arguably the most visited, photographed, and painted lighthouse in the country. Edward Hopper painted Portland Head Light in 1927; he also made several famous paintings of the lighthouse station at Two Lights in Cape Elizabeth and of the light on Monhegan Island. Painter Jamie Wyeth, son of Andrew Wyeth, lives and works in the lighthouse station on Southern Island off Tenants Harbor.

Once manned by stoic lighthouse keepers, all of Maine's lighthouses are now automated; yet in their lonely isolation they still evoke a sense of romance and heroism. Through its Maine Lights project, the Island Institute in Rockland has taken on the responsibility of finding civic and nonprofit organizations to assume ownership and maintenance of the lighthouse structures from the federal government. 🌲

Nubble Light at York Beach under a full moon. *Photo Ralph Morang*

Portland's Cultural Corridor

The recession that hit the Northeast during the late 1980s had a silver lining for downtown Portland. Real estate values plummeted so low that nonprofit arts groups were able to acquire former retail spaces and convert the heart of Maine's largest city into a cultural corridor.

Anchoring the Congress Street arts district is the 1983 Portland Museum of Art building designed by Henry Nichols Cobb of I. M. Pei & Partners. Next door, the Children's Museum of Maine took over the former chamber of commerce building. Just a block away, Maine College of Art converted what had been the city's largest department store, Porteous-Mitchell, into a state-of-the-art school complete with galleries, studios, library, and art supply store. The Maine Historical Society purchased the former Day's Jewelry Store, next to the Henry Wadsworth Longfellow House, and converted it into museum and exhibition space. Merrill Auditorium in Portland City Hall underwent a multimillion-dollar renovation, giving the Portland Symphony Orchestra a first-rate concert hall. And philanthropist Elizabeth B. Noyce capped off the downtown renaissance with the construction of the Portland Public Market, directly behind the public library.

Downtown Destinations

Center for Cultural Exchange,
  207-761-0591
Children's Museum of Maine,
  207-828-1234
Maine College of Art, Institute of
  Contemporary Art, 207-879-5742
Maine Historical Society,
  207-774-1822
Oak Street Theatre, 207-775-5103
Portland Concert Association,
  207-772-8630
Portland Museum of Art,
  207-775-6148
Portland Public Library,
  207-871-1700
Portland Public Market,
  207-772-8140
Portland Stage Company,
  207-774-1043
Portland Symphony Orchestra,
  207-773-6128
State Theatre, 207-879-1112
Wadsworth-Longfellow House,
  207-772-1807

"COUNTERBALANCING THE ECONOMIC STRESS OF THE area is a growing concentration of cultural institutions in this part of downtown Portland. The region's largest performing arts organizations and museums are located here, as is a significant population of artists working in all disciplines."

A Plan for Portland's Arts District, 1995

Above, top: The Children's Museum of Maine and the Portland Museum of Art are Congress Square neighbors. *Photo Brian Vanden Brink. Above, bottom:* The Old Port Festival celebrates the transformation of Portland's 19th-century mercantile district into a 20th-century entertainment district. *Photo Alan J. LaVallee*

Tom Clarity's political cartoon anticipated women's suffrage in 1920. Because Maine voted in September at the time, Maine women were the first to vote in a national election. *Maine State Museum, Augusta.* Right: James G. Blaine (1830–93) was a powerful U.S. senator, secretary of state, and 1884 presidential candidate during the Republican ascendancy of the 19th century. *Library of Congress*

"As Maine goes, so goes the nation."

Popular political slogan, c. 1888

In the 19th century, Maine held one of the nation's first primary elections, but the familiar "As Maine goes . . ." slogan also arose because America's political agenda in the 1880s was much influenced by powerful Maine men—Secretary of State James G. Blaine, Speaker of the House Thomas Brackett Reed, and acting Vice President William P. Frye among them. This tradition of statesmanship reached into the 20th century: Senator Edmund Muskie served as secretary of state, Senator William Cohen became secretary of defense, and Senator George Mitchell was named Senate majority leader and later brokered the peace accord in Northern Ireland.

Maine politicians tend to be commonsense moderates with an independent streak. Cohen, for example, often bucked his Republican Party, supporting Richard Nixon's impeachment and accepting a cabinet position in a Democratic administration. But the queen of Maine mavericks was Senator Margaret Chase Smith. The only woman in the U.S. Senate at the time, Maggie (as she was known back home) was the first political figure to stand up to Joseph McCarthy's Communist witch hunts. Maine is one

of the few states ever to be represented by two women in the U.S. Senate—Olympia Snowe and Susan Collins, both moderate Republicans. In 1992, despite being a longtime summer resident of Kennebunkport, then-President George Bush ran third in Maine behind Democrat Bill Clinton and Reform Party candidate H. Ross Perot (who won 30 percent of the vote, his highest percentage in any state).

Above: Victory by sculptor Bernard "Blackie" Langlais still stands in the late artist's farm pond in Cushing. *Frost Gully Archive. Left:* U.S. Senator Margaret Chase Smith, seen here greeting workers at a paper mill in 1960, was the first woman to serve in both houses of Congress and became famous for opposing McCarthyism. *Margaret Chase Smith Library, Skowhegan, Me.*

"THOSE OF US WHO SHOUT THE LOUDEST ABOUT Americanism in making character assassinations are all too frequently those who, by our words and acts, ignore some of the basic principles of Americanism: the right to criticize; the right to hold unpopular beliefs; the right to protest; the right of independent thought."

Senator Margaret Chase Smith, in her 1950 "Declaration of Conscience" speech in the U.S. Senate

An elegant example of the extended farm—big house, back house, little house, barn—in Brunswick. *Photo Brian Vanden Brink*

Dwelling in the Past

Even as Maine enters the 21st century, many of its residents still inhabit the 19th. The state's vernacular architecture is dominated by Federalist brick town houses and wooden homes of Greek Revival and Victorian influence. In rural Maine, the common and distinctive form is the connected farm, sometimes called "big house–little house–back house–barn." More than half of the pre-1900 buildings consist of a main house, kitchen ell, storage and work shed, and large barn. This style suited Maine's harsh climate, allowing farmers protected passage in winter, but the connected farm was also a model of practical efficiency when family farms were the backbone of the rural economy. 🌲

High Style Maine

While modesty is the hallmark of Maine design, the state has its share of historic mansions and villas. The most ostentatious is the Morse-Libby House, or Victoria Mansion, in downtown Portland. Designed by New Haven architect Henry Austin for hotel magnate Ruggles Sylvester Morse, the Victoria Mansion (1859–63) is considered the finest Italianate villa in the nation. From the asymmetrical massing of its brick-and-brownstone exterior to its ornately carved and painted interior, this Portland palace is the apotheosis of antebellum wealth. More representative of high-style Maine is Hamilton House, a large Georgian country house in South Berwick built for Portsmouth (New Hampshire) merchant Jonathan Hamilton in 1787–88. (Novelist and neighbor Sarah Orne Jewett used it as the setting of her 1901 novel *The Tory Lover*.) With its foursquare wooden rectitude, tall chimneys, and handsome dormered roof, Hamilton House is as lavish as colonial Maine ever got.

Above: The entry to the Morse-Libby House (Victoria Mansion) in Portland hints at the splendor to be found throughout. *Photo Brian Vanden Brink. Left:* The Lady Pepperell House (1760) in Kittery is considered one of the most sophisticated Georgian mansions in the United States. *Photo Brian Vanden Brink*

The coast of Maine is dotted with variations of the Shingle Style cottage, a style that brings order to complexity and speaks to ideals of comfort, leisure, and gentility. Between the 1880s and World War I, Shingle Style summer colonies popped up like mushrooms from York Harbor, Prouts Neck, and Cushing Island to Camden, Bar Harbor, and Grindstone Neck.
Photo Brian Vanden Brink

Great Shingled Arks

The building type perhaps most associated with Maine is the Shingle Style cottage, which came into vogue in the 1880s. Clad all in shingles with small windows and pitched, gabled roofs, these spacious "cottages" weathered well and became symbols of the good life along the coast. Boston architect William Ralph Emerson designed some of the first Shingle Style cottages for wealthy summer folk on Mount Desert Island, but Portland architect John Calvin Stevens was the chief proponent of the Shingle Style in Maine.

"SIMPLEST, MOST UNGARNISHED OF ALL, YET in many respects lovely, is life in the towns which are scattered along the seacoast, among the farm-lands, and along the southern borders of the vast forests. Here abound dwellings which express in a simple, primitive fashion, more or less graceful, the idea of home-comfort."

John Calvin Stevens and Albert Winslow Cobb, Examples of American Domestic Architecture, *1889*

Above: The Shingle Style writ large was the preferred look of the seaside inn. Here workers pose for a picture upon completing the Passaconaway on the Cape Neddick River in 1893. *Old York Historical Society. Left:* The c. 1905 Frederick E. Gignoux cottage in Cape Elizabeth was one of architect John Calvin Stevens's major Shingle Style creations of the 20th century. *Photo Bret Morgan*

Island Gardens

Some of Maine's most beautiful gardens thrive in the thin soil of its many islands. Poet Celia Thaxter's famous garden on Appledore, one of the Isles of Shoals, is geographically in Maine, but Thaxter was a resident of nearby Portsmouth, and thus New Hampshire has as much aesthetic claim to it. Thaxter and painter Childe Hassam immortalized her garden in their 1894 classic *An Island Garden.*

One of the greatest concentrations of public gardens is on Mount Desert Island. Jordan Pond House, a popular restaurant in Acadia National Park, features splendid flower gardens for cutting and decoration. Asticou Azalea Garden, with its Zen garden of raked sand, was designed in 1957 by Charles Savage, who also directed the development of Asticou Terrace and Thuya Lodge—a formal garden designed by landscape architect Joseph Henry Curtis and left by him to the town of Northeast Harbor in 1928. Asticou Terrace includes some plants

The cottage garden at Hamilton House in South Berwick was added to the grounds of Maine's finest Colonial estate in 1907. *Smithsonian Institution, Archives of American Gardens, Washington, D.C., Garden Club of America Collection*

from Reef Point, the Bar Harbor estate of Beatrix Jones Farrand, one of America's great garden designers. Farrand had her gardens at Reef Point destroyed shortly before her death in 1959, but the lavish walled garden she created for Abby Aldrich Rockefeller in Seal Harbor still exists and is occasionally open to the public.

"EVERYONE WANTS TO BE HERE, AND MANY PEOPLE, ESPECIALLY FROM garden-loving parts of the south, are struck by the abundance of lush growth, the intense color of flowers, and the large size of even the common flowers scattered about in the humblest garden box."

Jordan Pond horticulturist Scott L. Hadley,
The Gardens & Flowers of Jordan Pond, 1993

In a Kennebunkport Garden by Abbott Fuller Graves, c. 1895. Graves brought his American Impressionist vision to bear on Kennebunkport after moving to the coastal village from Boston in 1895. *Courtesy Spanierman Gallery, LLC, N.Y.*

Handmade in Maine

Maine's handbuilt boats are perhaps the purest expressions of its natural, "woods-and-water" aesthetic. Indians traversed the densely forested interior in birch-bark canoes, and European explorers and settlers used bark canoes as well. By the 1870s, birch bark was scarce, so canoe makers such as E. M. White and Old Town Canoe began translating the bark designs into

Gil Gilpatrick is one of several Maine guides still building wooden canoes the old-fashioned way. *Courtesy Gil Gilpatrick*

wood and canvas. Fiberglass and plastic canoes eventually took over the market, but some fine canoe makers still work in wood. Indeed, Maine is the East Coast center of wooden boat–making. *WoodenBoat* magazine, published in Brooklin,

chronicles the ongoing tradition of wooden workboats and pleasure craft such as the elegant Friendship sloop and the venerable peapod, first built on North Haven.

Crafts of all kinds are a tradition here. Hooked rugs originated in Maine and the nearby Maritime Provinces. Pine Tree State artisans have long turned their bounty of wood into furniture both fine and fanciful, from classic Shaker designs to novelty pieces

This novel deer- and moose-horn chair, made by C. E. Fish of Jonesboro, c. 1920–30, was considered a hunter's good luck chair. *Maine State Museum, Augusta*

fashioned from deer and moose antlers. One of the most venerable traditions is the making of splint or split-ash baskets. Mic Mac, Passamaquoddy, Penobscot, and Maliseet basket makers continue to produce beautiful and utilitarian baskets, the best known of which are Mic Mac potato baskets and backpacks. As ash trees become scarce, split-ash baskets are as apt to turn up now in museums and galleries as in potato fields.

The double-ended peapod looks like a seagoing canoe and was once the watercraft of choice for Maine's lobster fleet. Today, that honor goes to round-bottomed, double-wedge-hulled lobster boats equipped with powerful marine diesel engines. The seaworthy and maneuverable lobster boat, with its small forward cabin, high prow, and flat transom, is the true workhorse of the Gulf of Maine.

This patchwork quilt was made in 1885 for the Rev. F. L. Brooks, a circuit-riding minister, by the Harrington Methodist Society. *Maine State Museum, Augusta*

"WAKING OR SLEEPING, I DREAM OF BOATS—USUALLY OF RATHER small boats under a slight press of sail."

E. B. White, "The Sea and the Wind That Blows" in Essays of E. B. White, *1977. The writer's son Joel was one of Maine's foremost wooden boat-builders.*

A good old-fashioned clambake means cooking lobsters and clams in seaweed right down on the shore. *Photo Corbis-Bettmann*

The taste of Maine is simple and straight from the sea and soil—no fancy sauces or elaborate preparations. It's an al fresco meal of shellfish, baked potatoes, and blueberry pie washed down with a pint from one of the state's two dozen microbreweries. Mainers steam or boil lobsters at home or eat them "in the rough" at lobster pounds that dot the coast, but purists prefer a real downeast clambake, with lobsters and soft-shell clams steamed in beds of seaweed over an open-pit fire on the beach, then dipped in melted butter. Potatoes from "up the County" are wrapped in tinfoil and baked in the embers. Wild blueberries from Washington County make excellent pies, cakes, or muffins, but downing them by the handful or with a drizzle of fresh cream is the finest kind of eating.

The taste of Maine is also the Italian sandwich, a meal-in-a-roll thought to have originated with Italian workmen in Portland and first sold there by Amato's Italian Sandwich Shop in 1902. Other places have their grinders, poorboys, hoagies, and subs, but the Maine Italian is distinguished by its use of a long, chewy yeast roll. Sold at sandwich shops all over Maine, it is often the first thing a returning native craves. 🌲

A Real Maine Italian

Slice a loaf of Italian bread lengthwise to form a pocket. Insert strips of American cheese and boiled ham, thin slices of dill pickle, chopped onion and green pepper, wedges of tomato, and sliced black olives. Top with olive oil, salt and pepper to taste. (Italian sandwich shops then partially wrap the sandwich in lightweight butcher's paper, slice it in two, finish rolling it up, and secure the whole with a rubber band.)

Fresh blueberries and other fruits and vegetables make for a delicious outdoor Maine meal.
Kevin Shields

Whitewater rafting attracts thrill seekers to the Kennebec River, here at Magic Falls. *Photo Alan J. LaVallee*
Below: Maine is a fisher's paradise, whether an angler prefers bait, fly, surf-casting, or ice fishing. *Photo David Brownell*

Playing on the Water

Summer is a time for Mainers and visitors alike to get out and play on the water. The coast, lakes, and rivers that encouraged exploration and settlement are now the state's chief recreational assets. In northern Maine, the Allagash Wilderness Waterway, a 92-mile-long chain of

lakes and rivers, attracts 16,000 canoeists a year. The Allagash offers paddlers everything from flatwater lakes to swift rapids, and wildlife abounds. Thrill seekers come to ride Maine's whitewater in rubber rafts; rafting outfitters, most based in and around The Forks at the confluence of the Kennebec and Dead Rivers, guide thousands down the roiling waters of the Kennebec, the Penobscot, and the Dead.

People who can afford to be anywhere in the world sail the Maine coast in July and August. Whole families cruise the world-class sailing waters of Penobscot Bay and Casco Bay in search of adventure or just a place where they can anchor and escape the hectic pace of life ashore. Schooners out of Camden and Boothbay Harbor take boatloads of sightseers out onto the cold green waters of the North Atlantic for a taste of salt air and glimpses of whales, seals, and seabirds. ♣

Group of Boats (Watching the Regatta) **by Maurice Brazil Prendergast,** 1907. *Portland Museum of Art, Me. Photo by Melville D. McLean*

Robert Skoglund, the Humble Farmer, mixes dry Maine humor with hot jazz on his popular Maine Public Radio show. *Courtesy Robert Skoglund*

You Can't Get There from Here

Maine's tradition of storytelling goes back to Abenaki legends and the tall tales of lumber camps, spawning a literary legacy that includes the political satire of Seba Smith, the cracker-barrel philosophy of Artemus Ward, the local-color stories and poetry of Holman Day, and the wry humor of John Gould. But the oral tradition carries on, its best-known mani-festation being the "Bert & I" stories recorded and performed by Marshall Dodge and Robert Bryan. These classics of downeast humor poke gentle fun at folks from away while portraying Maine natives as commonsensical, literal-minded, and just a tad provincial. A chestnut of downeast humor has a tourist asking a local farmer, "Where does this road go?" "This road don't go nowhere," replies the farmer. "It mostly just sets right here." In a related classic, the local deadpans, in response to a tourist's request for directions, "You can't get there from here." This vein of Maine humor is now mined by comic storytellers such as Tim Sample, Robert Skoglund, and John MacDonald. The late Marshall Dodge founded the annual Maine Festival of the Arts, which helps keep downeast storytelling alive.

A Bit of "Bert & I"

A typical "Bert & I" joke goes something like this:

"What you so het up about?" one old chum asks another.

"Had to shoot my dog."

"Was he mad?"

"Well, he weren't too darned pleased."

A "Bert & I" record label

THE RETURN OF BERT AND I
MARSHALL DODGE
ROBERT BRYAN

Stereophonic   Side 2

1. By a Fluke
2. The Silent Chain Saw
3. Mam Hackett's Compost Heap
4. At the Graveyard
5. The Stove With the Powerful Draft
6. The Captain and the Lady
7. The Chicken Truck
8. Harry Startles Wiscasset

9 (BI 9-B)

Made in U.S.A.
Distributed By BERT & I, INC.,
Mill Road, Ipswich, Mass. 01938
BERT & I, INC. ©, copyright 1961

The entrance to the L. L. Bean retail store in Freeport has no locks, because the store is open 24 hours a day, 365 days a year. *Photo Brian Vanden Brink Opposite:* An early copy of L. L. Bean's popular mail-order catalogue. *L. L. Bean, Inc. Freeport, Me.*

"The Store That Knows the Outdoors"

Maine is an outdoor state, yet, truth be told, the number-one tourist activity is not hunting, fishing, hiking, sailing, skiing, or canoeing. It's shopping. And the number-one place to shop in Maine is L. L. Bean, "The Store That Knows the Outdoors." Founded in Freeport in 1912 by Leon Leonwood Bean, the emporium quickly established a reputation among sportsmen with the Maine Hunting Shoe—the famous "Bean Boot" Leon developed for wet-woods wear by stitching leather uppers to rubber bottoms. Today, L. L. Bean is a billion-dollar-a-year catalogue retail giant. Bean operators handle 15 million calls a year from around the globe, and the flagship store in Freeport is a 24-hour-a-day, 365-day-a-year shopping mecca. With 3.5 million visitors annually, L. L. Bean runs neck-and-neck with Acadia National Park as Maine's top tourist attraction. National chain stores looking to take advantage of the traffic generated by L. L. Bean have turned downtown Freeport into a retail outlet boomtown.

"SELL GOOD MERCHANDISE AT A reasonable profit, treat your customers like human beings, and they will always come back for more."

Leon Leonwood Bean's Golden Rule

Above: The Store That Knows the Outdoors and its catalogue empire were founded on sales of the eminently practical, always comfortable boot, and L. L. Bean now sells more than a quarter-million pairs each year. L. L. Bean, Inc. Freeport, Me.

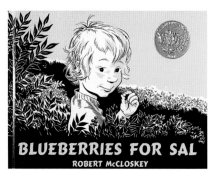

The Romance of Childhood

Maine's rich literary heritage begins with the literature of childhood, and that begins with poet Henry Wadsworth Longfellow, born in Portland in 1807 and educated at Bowdoin College. Generations of schoolchildren grew up reading Longfellow's epic "Song of Hiawatha," "Paul Revere's Ride," "Evangeline," and "The Courtship of Miles Standish" and memorizing shorter poems such as "The Wreck of the Hesperus," and "The Village Blacksmith."

In the 20th century, Bucks Harbor resident Robert McCloskey became an early master of the modern picture book with such classics of Maine summer life as *One Morning in Maine* and *Blueberries for Sal*. E. B. White's life on a saltwater farm in Brooklin informs his poignant masterpiece, *Charlotte's Web*. Margaret Wise Brown, best known for the enduring bedtime story *Goodnight, Moon*, was a sum-

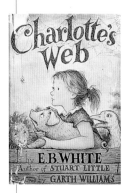

E. B. White's *Charlotte's Web* was inspired by spiders in White's North Brooklin barn and became one of the best-selling children's books of all time.

Above left: Blueberries for Sal by Robert McCloskey is the quintessential tale of innocence and experience on the coast of Maine.

mer resident of Vinalhaven, which she immortalized in *The Little Island*. Indeed, islands loom large in Maine's literary legacy. Barbara Cooney of Damariscotta, one of America's most honored author-illustrators, drew on the true story of a 19th-century Maine islander in *Island Boy*. 🍂

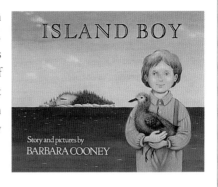

Above: Island Boy by award-winning author-illustrator Barbara Cooney was based on the life of Maine islander John Gilley. *Left:* Henry Wadsworth Longfellow's *Hiawatha* was a 19th-century best-seller. This undated illustration from a lantern slide shows the hero with Pearl Feather. *Corbis*

Longfellow heads a pantheon of Maine writers that stretches from Madam Wood—the state's first novelist, born in York in 1759—to Stephen King, the modern master of the macabre, born in Portland in 1947. Maine boasts three native-born Pulitzer prize–winning poets: Edna St. Vincent Millay, Edward Arlington Robinson, and Robert P. Tristram Coffin. It has also been the seasonal and adopted home of poets Robert Lowell, Robert Creeley, Philip Booth, and Amy Clampitt.

Outstanding prose writers include novelist Booth Tarkington, who summered at Kennebunkport, as did popular historical novelist Kenneth Roberts. E. B. White wrote his elegant essays from a saltwater farm on the

Blue Hill peninsula, not far from the homestead that back-to-the-land gurus Scott and Helen Nearing celebrated in *Living the Good Life.* A mecca for environmentalists, Maine has also nurtured such natural-history writers as Henry Beston, Rachel Carson, Frank Graham, and Franklin Burroughs. 🌲

Poet Edna St. Vincent Millay. *Culver Pictures*

OFTEN I THINK OF THE BEAUTIFUL TOWN
  That is seated by the sea;
Often in thought go up and down
The pleasant streets of that dear old town,
  And my youth comes back to me.

From "My Lost Youth," by Portland native
Henry Wadsworth Longfellow, 1858

Above: **Poet Henry Wadsworth Longfellow, in a daguerreotype by Southworth and Hawes, c. before 1855.** *The Metropolitan Museum of Art, New York.* *Left:* **Poet Robert Lowell lived in Castine when he was married to fellow writer Elizabeth Hardwick.** *Nancy Crampton/Farrar, Straus and Giroux*

"CERTAINLY MAINE HOMESTEADERS HAVE LITTLE OR NO HOPE TO 'strike it rich' as prospectors did in the early days in California or more recently in Alaska. Instead, they can work out a program that may give them a simple livelihood in exchange for a minimum of consistent and persistent work."

Helen and Scott Nearing, Continuing the Good Life, *1979*

Maine's Women Writers

Author Sarah Orne Jewett standing in the doorway of her South Berwick home. *Corbis-Bettmann*

Maine literary history is unusually deep in strong women writers. Harriet Beecher Stowe's *Pearl of Orr's Island* inspired the writing career of Sarah Orne Jewett, whose *Country of the Pointed Firs* became a classic of regional literature and spawned a whole sorority of Maine scene writers— among them Kate Douglas Wiggin, Elizabeth Ogilvie, Gladys Hasty Carroll, Elizabeth Coatsworth, and Ruth Moore. Among the more exotic imports have been novelist Marguerite Yourcenar, poet-memoirist May Sarton, and novelist and short-story writer Ann Beattie. The current queen of Maine writers is native-born Carolyn Chute, whose *Beans of Egypt, Maine* shone a harsh light on the state's rural poverty and triggered a debate about how well the "real Maine" was represented in its literature.

"THIS IS HOME. THE KIDS LIKE IT HERE. I LIKE IT HERE. We've lived here long enough that everybody's seen us. It's like shoes. It takes a while to break them in, but once you've broken them in, they're comfortable."

Stephen King on why he continues to live in Bangor, from a 1986 interview

The King of Horror

When *Carrie,* Stephen King's first horror novel, became a bestseller in 1973, no one could have guessed that over the next quarter century this strange young man from Maine would become one of the most successful writers of all time.

Maine's master of the macabre, Stephen King. *Photofest*

Year after year, Stephen King's creepy creations continue to scare and sell—*Salem's Lot, The Shining, The Stand, Cujo, Christine, Pet Sematary, Misery, Needful Things*—on and on. By giving imaginative expression to our deepest fears, King became a cultural force. His writings translate easily to the screen, and many of his books have become successful movies. But despite worldwide celebrity and fabulous wealth, he has remained a down-home boy, living and working in an old mansion in Bangor. There he has made himself Public Citizen number one, contributing largely to public library renovations, the YMCA, the University of Maine in nearby Orono (his alma mater), and building local kids a baseball stadium familiarly known as the Field of Screams.

Of Folkies, Straw Hats, and Hollywood

Above: A scene from the 1957 Jerry Wald production of *Peyton Place,* filmed in Camden. *John Springer/Corbis. Below:* Noel Paul Stookey (to the left of Mary Travers and Peter Yarrow) made a name for himself as part of the Peter, Paul and Mary folk trio and a home for himself in Brooklin, Maine. *Photofest. Opposite:* Shirley Jones and Gordon MacRae starred in the 20th Century Fox production of *Carousel,* filmed in Boothbay Harbor. *John Springer/Corbis*

Maine's profile is not as high in the performing arts as in literature or painting, but it has its lively side. Singer Rudy Vallee, who grew up in Westbrook, made "The Maine Stein Song" the country's top hit in 1930. Musical preferences run toward folk and country music: Noel Paul Stookey, of Peter, Paul & Mary fame, has lived on the Blue Hill peninsula for many years; his henhouse served as the first studio of Maine's community radio station, WERU (We Are You). Country-western singer Dick Curless and folkies Gordon Bok and Dave Mallett are native sons.

Theater is largely summer fare. Vacationland's straw-hat circuit includes the Ogunquit Playhouse, Lakewood Theatre,

Maine State Music Theater, and the Theater at Monmouth. The movie industry has only lately discovered the state's beauties; for decades, the only major films made here were *Carousel,* shot in Boothbay, and *Peyton Place,* in Camden. More recently several Stephen King projects, including *Pet Sematary,* and other features have been filmed in Maine. Superstar John Travolta maintains a summer home on Islesboro, as did Kirstie Alley. Maine's most important Hollywood figure, though, was Academy Award–winning director John Ford (*Stagecoach, The Grapes of Wrath*), born John Feeney in Portland in 1895.

Reel-Life Maine

Way Down East (1920) D. W. Griffith melodrama; Lillian Gish swept down a Maine river on an ice floe

Carousel (1956) Screen adaptation of Rodgers & Hammerstein musical with Shirley Jones and Gordon MacRae

Peyton Place (1957) Grace Metalious's best-seller about scandalous small-town lives

Sunrise at Campobello (1960) FDR battles polio, set in Roosevelt's summer home on the Canadian border

Carrie (1976) Sissy Spacek and John Travolta in Stephen King's scary tale of a small-town misfit

On Golden Pond (1981) Henry Fonda's last movie, inspired by Maine's Belgrade Lake (but filmed in New Hampshire)

Man Without a Face (1993) Tale of friendship between a lonely boy and reclusive ex-teacher, shot in Rockport and Deer Isle; Mel Gibson starred and directed

Message in a Bottle (1998) Kevin Costner romantic vehicle, filmed in various Maine towns

Lake Placid (1999) Alligator creature feature starring Bridget Fonda, set on a northern Maine lake (but shot in Canada)

The artist most closely linked with Maine is Winslow Homer (1836–1910). Born in Boston, Homer made a name as an illustrator during the Civil War, settled in New York for his middle years, and became one of America's foremost watercolorists. Following a trip to England's rugged North Sea coast in 1881–82, the sea became Homer's consuming passion, so in 1883 he moved to a wild and beautiful promontory in Scarborough

known as Prouts Neck. There, in a cottage studio within reach of the salt spray, he lived out his days, painting the many moods of the sea and coastal skies in naturalistic oils that have inspired generations of viewers and artists. Homer defined "Maine art" as an elemental response to nature's power and established the archetype of the Maine realist closely attuned to the natural world.

In 1983, a century after Homer came to Prouts Neck, the Portland Museum of Art opened its Charles Shipman Payson building, the gift of a local industrialist who felt the museum needed a suitable home for the 17 Homers he had previously given. ▲

Winslow Homer working on *Gulf Stream* in his Prouts Neck studio, 1899. Homer's studio is now surrounded by a gated summer colony but is still available to scholars and admirers on a limited basis. *Bowdoin College Museum of Art, Brunswick. Left: Right and Left* by Winslow Homer, 1909. *National Gallery of Art, Washington, D.C. Opposite above: The Herring Net* by Winslow Homer, 1885. *The Art Institute of Chicago. Opposite below: The West Wind* by Winslow Homer, 1891. *Addison Gallery of American Art, Phillips Academy, Andover, Massachusetts*

"THE LIFE THAT I HAVE CHOSEN GIVES ME MY FULL HOURS OF ENJOY-ment for the balance of my life. The Sun will not rise, or set, without my notice, and thanks."

Winslow Homer in a letter to his brother, February 1895

Maine—Jordan's Delight Island by John Marin, 1935. *Christie's Images Below: City of Bath* by Marguerite Zorach, c. 1927. Marguerite Zorach and her sculptor husband William helped bring the modernist aesthetic to Maine. *Farnsworth Art Museum, Rockland*

Maine truly came into its own as an artists' mecca just after the turn of the century with the modernists, who aimed to replace objective imitation of nature with subjective self-expression. This aesthetic sea change was brought to Maine by patron-critic Hamilton Easter Field, who founded the Ogunquit art colony. Influential painter and teacher Robert Henri started another colony on Monhegan Island, where George Bellows, Edward Hopper, Leon Kroll, and Rockwell Kent came to paint. Sculptor William Zorach and painter Marguerite Zorach settled in Robinhood.

Maine's twin pillars of modernism were John Marin and Marsden Hartley. Marin painted up and down the coast but eventually settled downeast, on Cape Split in Washington County, where he painted the sea with a dynamic expressionism bordering on abstraction. Hartley, Maine's one true native genius, was born in Lewiston and roamed the world, sampling the major art movements of the early 20th century. In his final years, Hartley landed in the downeast fishing village of Corea, where he made powerful symbolic paintings from his native experience. ▲

Maine Snowstorm by Marsden Hartley, 1908. Hartley spent the stormy winter of 1908–9 alone in a cabin in North Lovell. *Frederick R. Weisman Art Museum, University of Minnesota*

"I AM COMPLETELY RECOGNIZED as an authentic painter of Maine born in Maine, but this recognition comes I am happy to say from the state itself and the native spirit which recognizes the authenticity of my private and local emotion."

Marsden Hartley, *"Is There an American Art?"* c. 1938

Abstraction is an urban impulse and Maine is a rural state. Realism is the bedrock of Maine art, from Winslow Homer's storm-tossed seas to Edward Hopper's lonely lighthouses to Rockwell Kent's heroic images of Monhegan

fishermen. So while the mainstream of American art has flowed in other directions, painterly realism remains the coin of this realm. Fairfield Porter, also an important critic, painted his sunny views of summer life on Great Spruce Head, the island his family still owns in Penobscot Bay. Neil Welliver, perhaps America's greatest living landscapist, lives and works on a farm in Lincolnville, not far

Above: Island Farmhouse by Fairfield Porter, 1969. Porter was not only a fine painterly realist, he was also an influential art critic who saw the beauty in both representational and abstract art. *Private collection, Cleveland*

Christina's World by Andrew Wyeth, 1948. This image of the crippled spinster Christina Olson crawling back to her house from the family graveyard may well be the most famous American painting of the 20th century. *The Museum of Modern Art, New York.* Opposite bottom: *Monhegan, Maine* by Rockwell Kent, c. 1947. Kent cut his eyeteeth as an artist on Monhegan at the turn of the century, but this stark vision was painted upon his return as a mature artist. *Colby College Museum of Art, Waterville, Me.*

from the summer studio of his friend Alex Katz, the well-known figurative realist.

Then there are the Wyeths. Famed illustrator N. C. Wyeth brought his young family to Port Clyde in the 1920s, and son Andrew Wyeth and grandson Jamie Wyeth continue to paint the secrets of the Maine coast from their own private islands. The Olson House, where Andrew painted *Christina's World*—perhaps the most famous modern American painting—attracts visitors from all over the world. In 1998, the Farnsworth Museum in Rockland opened a new wing devoted exclusively to the Maine works of the Wyeth family. 🌲

Until the 1970s, most of the art produced in Maine was made by summer residents and artists "from away." Since then, however, quite a few native and adopted Mainers have made their mark. Among natives, Alan Bray paints interior Maine landscapes with a unique strangeness that draws from folk art and the Renaissance. Dozier Bell internalizes the landscape to produce dark visions that are part memory, part apocalypse. North Haven islander Eric Hopkins paints highly streamlined coastal views, often with an aerial perspective. Charlie Hewitt, traveling between New York and Vinalhaven, brings urban expres-

Mount Kineo by Alan Bray, 1997. Alan Bray is a Maine native who studied art in Italy and then returned to Dover-Foxcroft, where he creates images of the Maine landscape that have an almost otherworldly quality. *Schmidt Bingham Gallery*

sionism to Maine subjects. And sculptor Celeste Roberge creates works in stacked stone and welded steel that give concrete expression to conceptual realities.

Several outstanding abstract artists live in Maine, among them Abby Shahn, Frederick Lynch, and Alison Hildreth—but realism remains king. Alan Magee was a highly regarded illustrator before he turned his brush to impossibly photorealistic images of Maine beach stones.

South Bristol Harbor by Connie Hayes, 1997. Connie Hayes has carved out a niche for herself as a house-sitting artist. Art lovers all over Maine have allowed her to stay in their homes and cottages in exchange for paintings. *Greenhut Gallery, Portland, Me.*

Brett Bigbee paints painstaking, iconic images of himself and his family. Mark Wethli at Bowdoin College and Joseph Nicoletti at Bates College are sublime still-life artists. DeWitt Hardy makes sensuous watercolors of sleepy backwater towns along the Maine–New Hampshire border. And Marguerite Robichaux, who lives and works in the western Maine mountains, paints what amounts to a visual diary of the state's natural treasures. ♣

Red Laundry in Woods by Lois Dodd, 1979. Lois Dodd summers just down the road from the Olson House in Cushing and was responsible for bringing Alex Katz and other realist painters to Maine. *Fischbach Gallery.* © *Lois Dodd/Licensed by VAGA, New York, N.Y.* Right: *Matrix #8: Tide* by Dozier Bell, 1995. Dozier Bell grew up in Lewiston. Her work, combining photography and painting, tends to be dark and brooding. *Schmidt Bingham Gallery*

Counterform #41 by Frederick Lynch, 1998. One of Maine's best abstract artists, Lynch began exploring the stripe motif in the 1970s while painting human figures wearing striped shirts. *McGowan Fine Art.*

The Maine Art Tour

While nature is Maine's big draw, cultural tourism has become very popular. Several arts and crafts schools take advantage of the fact.

Skowhegan School of Painting & Sculpture (207-474-9345)
Highly competitive summer school

Haystack Mountain School of Crafts (207-348-2306)
One of the country's premier summer crafts schools; Deer Isle

Watershed Center for the Ceramic Arts (207-882-6075)
Nonprofit residency program for ceramic artists; Newcastle

Center for Furniture Craftsmanship (207-594-5611)
Offers 2-week and 12-week courses in furniture design and building; Rockport

Maine Photographic Workshop (207-236-8581)
Courses for amateur and professional photographers; Rockport

WoodenBoat School (207-359-4651)
Teaches the art of building wooden boats; Brooklin

Mother Eartha

Eartha, the world's largest globe, rotates on its axis in the lobby of the DeLorme Mapping Company headquarters in Yarmouth. Measuring 42 feet in diameter and 130 feet in circumference, Eartha attracts lots of visitors to the company store, which sells paper maps and atlases as well as DeLorme's digital maps.

Going Native in a Big Way

Sculptor Bernard "Blackie" Langlais created Skowhegan's landmark wooden Indian in 1969 to honor the original inhabitants of the region. Standing 62 feet above its base, Langlais's carved and carpentered Indian holds a spear in one hand and a fishing net in the other.

His Ears Must Be Burning

A favorite son of the town of Farmington, Chester Greenwood invented the earmuff in 1873—when he was only 15—by combining beaver fur, velvet, and wire. Farmington celebrates young Chester's contribution to culture each December with a day of parades, polar bear swims, and general merriment.

Eat My Wake

Lobster boats are essentially seagoing pickup trucks, and lobster boat races are the maritime equivalent of drag races. The granddaddy of them all is the World's Fastest Lobsterboat Race, held in Jonesport each Fourth of July amidst barbecues, beauty pageants, and fireworks.

Perham's Rocks

Perham's of West Paris, in business since 1919, is Maine's mineralogy mecca. Part rock shop, part jewelry store, and part gem museum, Perham's attracts prospectors and collectors from all over the globe to the Oxford Hills, the state's premier rockhounding region. The emporium provides maps to open mines and quarries.

Angus, King of the Mountain

The world's tallest snowman, as recognized by the Guinness Book of Records, was built in the winter resort of Bethel in February 1999. At 113 feet 7 inches and 9 million pounds, the ten-story snowman was named after Maine Governor Angus King. There are no plans to reincarnate Angus, but between December 25, 1999, and February 19, 2000, Bethel plans to mark the millennium by erecting 2,000 snowmen.

Save the Furbish Lousewort!

A wild snapdragon, the Furbish lousewort grows nowhere else in the world except on the banks of the St. John River. It was discovered in 1880 by amateur botanist and natural history artist Kate Furbish (1834–1931) of Brunswick. A century later, the presence of this rare plant played a key role in defeating a proposed dam project that would have flooded 88,000 acres in the St. John Valley.

Great People

A selective listing of Mainers, native and adopted, concentrating on the arts.

Rudy Vallee (1901–1986), singer

Berenice Abbott (1898–1992), photographer; famous for pictures of Maine and New York and for rediscovering French photographer Eugene Atget

Rachel Carson (1907–1964), author, naturalist; sounded the alarm about pesticide pollution in *Silent Spring*

Carolyn Chute (b. 1947), novelist

Robert P. Tristram Coffin (1892–1955), poet, Bowdoin professor; won 1935 Pulitzer Prize for *Strange Holiness*

John Ford (1895–1973), film director

Marsden Hartley (1877–1943), artist

Winslow Homer (1836–1910), painter

Robert Indiana (b. 1928), Pop artist, famous for LOVE design

Sarah Orne Jewett (1849–1909), novelist and short-story writer

Rockwell Kent (1882–1971), painter, author-illustrator: *It's Me, O Lord, Greenland Journal*

Stephen King (b. 1947), novelist

Henry Wadsworth Longfellow (1807–1882), poet of American epics

John Marin (1870–1953), artist

Gary Merrill (1915–1990), actor, was married to actress Bette Davis

Edna St. Vincent Millay (1892–1950), Pulitzer prize–winning poet

Ruth Moore (1903–1989), novelist, author of *Spoonhandle, The Weir, Candlemas Bay*

Kenneth Roberts (1885–1957), writer, won special Pulitzer Prize in 1957 for his historical novels

Edwin Arlington Robinson (1869–1935), Pulitzer Prize–winning poet; wrote "Richard Corey," "Miniver Cheevy"

John Calvin Stevens (1855–1940), architect, popularized Shingle Style

E. B. White (1899–1985), author and essayist: *One Man's Meat, Charlotte's Web*

N. C. Wyeth (1882–1945), artist-illustrator, patriarch of painter clan

Andrew Wyeth (b. 1917), painter

Marguerite Yourcenar (1903–1987), writer, *Memoirs of Hadrian, The Abyss;* member of the French Academy; year-round resident of Northeast Harbor

. . . and Great Places

Some interesting derivations of Maine place names

Airline Somewhat ironic local designation for Route 9 between Brewer and Calais. Bucking through one of Maine's wildest areas, the Airline is one of the state's few east–west highways.

Allagash From the Wabanaki word for "bark cabin."

Blue Hill Coastal town named for landmark hill that appears blue-black from a distance owing to spruce and fir.

Calais Named for the French city but pronounced *CAL-is.*

Caribou Named for reindeer species that once roamed northern Maine.

Flagstaff Lake The manmade lake and the town it inundated in 1949 take their name from the flagpole Benedict Arnold erected there in 1775 on his ill-fated march to Quebec.

The Forks Settlement where the Dead and Kennebec Rivers converge.

Kokadjo From Wabanaki for "kettle." Abenaki demon Glooskap supposedly dropped his kettle here while pursuing the calf of a moose he had killed.

Mars Hill In 1790, a British chaplain with a survey crew preached a sermon here, citing a biblical passage about the hill in Athens sacred to the god of war.

Meddybemps From the Wabanaki words for "plenty of alewives."

Moosehead Lake So named because its outline resembles an antlered moose head.

Mount Desert Island Samuel de Champlain in 1604 named this top tourist attraction "L'isle de Monts Desert" because of its barren mountains.

Mount Katahdin Mile-high peak that takes its name from the Wabanaki word for "greatest mountain."

Mount Kineo Mountain in the middle of Moosehead Lake named for a Wabanaki chief and, according to myth, actually a moose Glooskap killed.

Saco City takes its name from Wabanaki for "outlet of the river" and is pronounced *SOCK-o.*

Vienna Town named after Austrian city but pronounced with a long "i," *Vi-ENNA.*

Wytopitlock Rural settlement takes its name from the Wabanaki word for "place where there are alders."

Cadillac Mountain For Antoine de Lamothe Cadillac, the first to be granted land in the area by the king of France.

MAINE BY THE SEASONS
A Perennial Calendar of Events and Festivals

Here is a selective listing of events that take place each year in the months noted;
we suggest calling ahead to local chambers of commerce for dates and details.

January

Rangeley
   Rangeley Sno-de-o
   A weekend of snowmobile
   races, parades, and parties

Sugarloaf/Carrabasset Valley
   White, White World Week
   Fireworks, parades, music, and,
   of course, skiing

February

Bridgton
   Musher's Bowl
   Sled dog races

Camden
   National Toboggan Championships

Madawaska
   International Snowmobilers Festival
   Events on both sides of the
   Maine–Canada border

March

Fort Kent
   Can-Am Crown Sled Dog Races

Island Falls
   Log Driver's Cookout
   Snow sledders' cookout at Mud
   Pond featuring "World's Largest
   Coffee Pot"

Statewide
   Maine Maple Sunday

April

Boothbay Harbor
   Fishermen's Festival
   Lobster-trap hauling competitions, tug-o-war, clam-shuck-
   ing contests; a local celebration
   for locals before tourist season

Portland
   Aucocisco
   Ten-day environmental and
   cultural celebration of Casco
   Bay
   Patriot's Day Road Race

May

Greenville
   Moosemainea
   Monthlong celebration of
   moose; parades, crafts, races,
   mountain biking, family fun

Lewiston/Auburn
   Maine State Parade
   Maine's largest parade

Unity
   Fiddlehead Festival
   Celebration of fiddlehead fern
   harvest

June

Bethel–Rockport
   *Trek Across Maine—Sunday
   River to the Sea*
   Three-day, 180-mile bicycle ride

(not a race) to benefit the
Maine Lung Association

Biddeford
   La Kermesse
   Franco-American festival in heav-
   ily Franco-American mill town

Boothbay Harbor
   Annual Windjammer Days
   Music, fireworks, and food on
   the annual gathering of windjammer sloops

Madawaska
   Acadian Festival
   Celebration of the French-
   Canadian culture of the St.
   John Valley

Portland
   Old Port Festival
   Street festival in Portland's
   quaint waterfront district

July

Augusta
   Whatever Family Festival
   Annual celebration of the
   clean-up of the Kennebec River

Bar Harbor
   Bar Harbor Music Festival
   *Downeast Dulcimer and Folk Harp
   Festival*

Bethel
   Mollyockett Day

Foot races, fiddling competitions, and a parade honoring a locally famous Indian woman

Fort Fairfield
Maine Potato Blossom Festival
Aroostook County celebration of its cash crop

Lewiston
Bates Dance Festival
Bates College invites important modern dancers each summer to perform and teach

Lisbon Falls
Moxie Festival
Celebration of the soft drink

Rockland
Schooner Days

Union
Full Circle Summer Fair
New Age festival of arts and crafts

Yarmouth
Yarmouth Clam Festival
Clams, crafts, and carnival rides top the bill in one of the state's largest summer festivals

August

Bangor
Bangor State Fair

Brunswick
Maine Festival of the Arts
The state's premier celebration of local arts and crafts

Maine Highland Games
Traditional Scottish sporting events and bagpipers

Calais
International Festival
Celebration of friendship between Calais and neighboring St. Stephen, New Brunswick

Lewiston
Great Falls Balloon Festival
Hot air balloon festival

Machias
Wild Blueberry Festival
Washington County celebration of its cash crop

Rockland
Maine Lobster Festival
Big harborside celebration of succulent seafood

Skowhegan
Skowhegan State Fair

Union
Union Fair

Windsor
Windsor Fair

September

Bangor
Paul Bunyan Festival Days
Entertainment, foods, crafts, children's events

Blue Hill
Blue Hill Fair
One of the best old-time country fairs

Cumberland
Cumberland Fair

Freedom
Healing Arts Festival

Holistic celebration of peace, unity, and spiritual renewal

Greenville
International Seaplane Fly-In
Contests, bomb drops, and demonstrations of bush-piloting skills on Moosehead Lake

Litchfield
Litchfield Fair

Oxford
Oxford County Fair

Unity
Common Ground Country Fair
Maine's alternative (and best) agricultural fair

October

Camden
Fall Festival of Arts and Crafts

Fryeburg
Fryeburg Fair
Maine's largest and most popular agricultural fair

November

Statewide
Deer hunting season

Christmas crafts fairs
Most major towns and cities

December

Farmington
Chester Greenwood Day
Parade and events honoring the inventor of the ear muff

Portland
New Year's Portland
Maine's biggest New Year's party

WHERE TO GO
Museums, Attractions, Gardens, and Other Arts Resources

Call for seasons and hours when open.

Museums

ABBE MUSEUM
Sieur de Monts Springs, Acadia National Park, 207-288-3519
Private museum with a collection of 50,000 prehistoric and historic Native American artifacts.

BATES COLLEGE MUSEUM OF ART
141 Nichols St., Lewiston, 208-786-6158
Small college gallery and museum with an important collection of Marsden Hartley art and memorabilia.

BOWDOIN COLLEGE MUSEUM OF ART
Walker Art Building, Brunswick, 207-725-3275
Maine's oldest art museum with deep, general collection housed in a McKim, Mead & White building.

BRICK STORE MUSEUM
117 Main St., Kennebunk, 207-985-4802
Excellent local history museum with focus on the social, cultural, and maritime history of the Kennebunks.

CHILDREN'S MUSEUM OF MAINE
142 Free St., Portland, 207-828-1234
An interactive discovery museum for young people.

COLBY COLLEGE MUSEUM OF ART
5600 Mayflower Hill Dr., Waterville, 207-872-3228
Fast-growing major academic art museum with focus on American art; special collections of works by John Marin and Alex Katz.

FARNSWORTH MUSEUM OF ART
352 Main St., Rockland, 207-596-6457
Excellent regional museum with focus on Maine and American art; opened Farnsworth Center for the Wyeth Family in Maine in 1998.

MAINE HISTORICAL SOCIETY
485–489 Congress St., Portland, 207-879-0427
Extensive library, new exhibition galleries, and Wadsworth-Longfellow House make this ground zero for Maine history research.

MAINE MARITIME MUSEUM
243 Washington St., Bath, 207-443-1316
Maine's biggest and best marine museum; maintains former Percy & Small Shipyard; located on Kennebec River.

MAINE STATE MUSEUM
State House Complex, Augusta, 207-287-2301
The industrial, archaeological, and natural history of Maine in well-designed exhibitions.

OGUNQUIT MUSEUM OF AMERICAN ART
183 Shore Rd., Ogunquit, 207-646-4909
Seaside museum, open summers only; mostly 20th-century art and artists associated with the Ogunquit art colony.

OLD YORK HISTORICAL SOCIETY
Lindsay Rd., York, 207-363-4974
Six colonial and post-colonial buildings with a research library and costumed interpreters.

PENOBSCOT MARINE MUSEUM
Church St. at Route 1, Searsport, 207-548-2529
Maine's oldest maritime museum; marine paintings, ship models, China trade objects.

PORTLAND MUSEUM OF ART
7 Congress Square, Portland, 207-775-6148
Maine's flagship art museum, rejuvenated in 1983 with opening of Charles Shipman Payson Wing designed by Henry N. Cobb of I. M. Pei and gift of 17 Winslow Homer paintings from the Payson collection.

Attractions

ACADIAN VILLAGE
Route 1, Van Buren, 207-868-5042
Two-and-a-half-acre exhibit of 16 antique and replica buildings re-creating Acadian settlement c. 1785.

GILSLAND FARM
Route 1, Falmouth, 207-781-2330
Maine Audubon Society's 60-acre headquarters; two miles of trails, salt marshes, meadows, woodlands, organic gardens, natural history displays, gift shop, and bookstore.

JONES MUSEUM OF GLASS AND CERAMICS
Douglas Mt. Rd., Sebago, 207-787-3370
Collection of some 8,000 pieces of antique glass and ceramics.

LAUDHOLM FARM
342 Laudholm Farm Rd., Wells, 207-646-1555
Saltwater farm headquarters of the Wells National Estuarine Research Reserve; 1,600 acres bordering Rachel Carson National Wildlife Refuge; naturalist tours; September nature crafts show.

NORDICA HOMESTEAD MUSEUM
Holley Rd., Farmington, 207-778-2042
Birthplace of Wagnerian diva Lillian Nordica, a must for opera buffs.

OWLS HEAD TRANSPORTATION MUSEUM
Route 73, Owls Head, 207-594-4418
On grounds of Knox County Airport, 60-acre campus is a motherlode of antique automobiles and airplanes.

PATTEN LUMBERMAN'S MUSEUM
Shin Pond Rd., Patten, 207-528-2650
Timber industry tales and technology in 10 buildings of open-air museum.

PEARY-MACMILLAN ARCTIC MUSEUM
Bowdoin College, Brunswick, 207-725-3416
Curious little museum of art and artifacts brought back from the Arctic by Robert Peary and Donald MacMillan.

ROOSEVELT-CAMPOBELLO INTERNATIONAL PARK
Campobello Island, New Brunswick, Canada, 506-752-2922
FDR's summer home, under joint U.S.–Canada jurisdiction; just across the bridge from Lubec.

SEASHORE TROLLEY MUSEUM
Log Cabin Rd., Kennebunkport, 207-967-2800
Over 200 trolleys, 4 miles of track, gift shop, snack bar.

SOUTHWORTH PLANETARIUM
University of Southern Maine, Portland, 207-780-4249
Laser light shows under a 30-foot domed "sky."

STANWOOD HOMESTEAD MUSEUM
Bar Harbor Rd., Ellsworth, 207-667-8460
Former home of ornithologist Cordelia Stanwood; period furniture, wildlife exhibitions, and 130-acre sanctuary.

WENDELL GILLEY MUSEUM OF BIRD CARVING
Herrick Rd., Southwest Harbor, 207-244-7555
Marvelous little museum featuring more than 200 wooden birds by master carver Wendell Gilley (1904–1983).

WILLOWBROOK AT NEWFIELD
Main St., Newfield, 207-793-2784
Nineteenth-century museum/village with 37 buildings filled with tools, toys, farm equipment, musical instruments; country store, schoolhouse, fire barn, carousel.

Homes and Gardens

THUYA LODGE AND ASTICOU TERRACE
Route 3, Northeast Harbor, 207-267-5130
Magical cottage and walled garden high above the harbor; inspired by Beatrix Farrand and designed by Charles K. Savage.

COLONEL BLACK MANSION

Route 172, Ellsworth

Remarkably preserved 1824–27 Federalist brick mansion, gardens, picnic spots, and 3 miles of walking trails.

JOSHUA L. CHAMBERLAIN MUSEUM

226 Maine St., Brunswick, 207-729-6606

Civil War hero's home maintained as house museum.

HAMILTON HOUSE

18 Vaughan's Lane, South Berwick, 207-384-5269

Large Georgian country house (1787–88) with colonial gardens; owned and maintained by the Society for the Preservation of New England Antiquities.

SARAH ORNE JEWETT HOUSE

5 Portland St., South Berwick, 207-384-2454

Author Sarah Orne Jewett did most of her writing in this 1774 Georgian-style house; also owned by SPNEA.

MONTPELIER

Corner of Routes 1 and 131, Thomaston, 207-354-8062

Reproduction of 1795 mansion once occupied by Revolutionary War Gen. Henry Knox.

NORLANDS LIVING HISTORY CENTER

290 Norlands Rd., Livermore, 207-897-4366

Elegantly restored farmstead of the politically powerful Washburn family; operated as a live-in history center to give students a taste of 19th-century rural life.

POWNALBOROUGH COURT HOUSE

River Rd., Dresden, 207-882-6817

John Adams once practiced law in Maine's oldest surviving judicial structure (1761), which sits high and handsome on the banks of the Kennebec River.

ABBY ALDRICH ROCKEFELLER GARDENS

Off Route 3, Seal Harbor, 207-276-3330

Exquisite walled garden designed by Beatrix Farrand; open by reservation only.

RUGGLES HOUSE

Main St., Columbia Falls, 207-483-4637

Regarded by experts as one of the world's grandest small houses, this 1820 Federalist residence features a flying staircase and intricately carved woodwork.

TATE HOUSE

1270 Westbrook St., Portland, 207-774-9781

Built in 1755 for the mast agent of the Royal Navy, this National Historic Landmark features a fine 18th-century herb garden.

VICTORIA MANSION

109 Danforth St., Portland, 207-772-4841

Also known as the Morse-Libby House; built between 1859 and 1863 and considered one of America's finest Italianate villas.

WADSWORTH-LONGFELLOW HOUSE

485 Congress St., Portland, 207-879-0427

Built in 1785-86, the childhood home of poet Henry Wadsworth Longfellow was the first brick home in Portland.

Other Resources

MAINE COAST ARTISTS

162 Russell Ave., Rockport, 207-236-2875

Nonprofit, noncollecting gallery; one of the best places to see contemporary Maine art.

MAINE COLLEGE OF ART

522 Congress St., Portland, 207-775-3052

Professional art school and Institute of Contemporary Art.

MAINE WRITERS & PUBLISHERS ALLIANCE

12 Pleasant St., Brunswick, 207-729-6333

Clearinghouse for Maine books.

CREDITS

The authors have made every effort to reach copyright holders of text and owners of illustrations, and wish to thank those individuals and institutions that permitted the reprinting of text or the reproduction of works in their collections. Credits not listed in the captions are provided below. References are to page numbers; the designations a, b, and c indicate position of illustrations on pages.

Illustrations

ADDISON GALLERY OF AMERICAN ART: **76b** *The West Wind.* Oil on canvas. 30 x 44". © Addison Gallery of American Art, gift of anonymous donor, Phillips Academy, Andover, Mass. All rights reserved. 1928.24; THE ART INSTITUTE OF CHICAGO **76a** *The Herring Net.* Oil on canvas. 30⅛ x 48⅜". Mr. and Mrs. Martin A. Ryerson Collection; BOWDOIN COLLEGE MUSEUM OF ART, BRUNSWICK, MAINE: **77a** Silver print photograph. Gift of the Homer Family; DAVID BROWNELL: **14b;** CHRISTIE'S IMAGES: **78a** *Maine—Jordan's Delight.* Watercolor, gouache, pen and ink on paper on board. 15 x 22"; COLBY COLLEGE MUSEUM OF ART: **80b** *Monhegan, Maine.* Oil on canvas. 28 x 44"; COLUMBUS MUSEUM OF ART, OHIO: **22** *The Swimmer.* Oil on canvas. 20½ x 30½". © Estate of Yasuo Kuniyoshi/Licensed by VAGA, New York, N.Y.; CORBIS-BETTMAN: **88;** BUZ CROCKER: **87;** DELORME/NANCE S. TRUEWORTHY: **86a;** TIBOR DE NAGY GALLERY, N.Y.: **27** *Sand Pool.* Oil on canvas. 72 x 72"; FARNSWORTH ART MUSEUM: **30–31** *A Morning View of Blue Hill Village.* Oil on canvas. 25⅝ x 52¼". Museum purchase, 1965. Photo Melville D. McLean; **78b** *City of Bath.* Oil on canvas. 18 x 30". Gift of Dahlov Ipcar and Tessim Zorach, 1986; FISHBACH GALLERY: **84a** *Red Laundry in Woods.* Oil on canvas. 48 x 40". © Lois Dodd/Licensed by VAGA, New York, N.Y.; FREDERICK R. WEISMAN ART MUSEUM, UNIVERSITY OF MINNESOTA: **79** *Maine Snowstorm.* Oil on canvas. 30⅛ x 30⅛". Gift of Ione and Hudson Walker; COLLECTION JOANN AND JULIAN GANZ: **8–9** *The Artist Sketching at Mount Desert.* Oil on canvas. 11 x 19"; GREATER FARMINGTON CHAMBER OF COMMERCE: **86b;** GREENHUT GALLERY: **83** *South Bristol Harbor.* Oil on canvas. 12 x 12"; COLLECTION OF HENRY AND JODY MCCORCLES: **11** *Culminating Lace of the Ferry Master's Garden.* Oil on canvas. 30 x 36"; MCGOWAN FINE ART: **85** *Counterform #41.* Oil on canvas on panel. 68 x 48"; THE METROPOLITAN MUSEUM OF ART, N.Y.: **25** *Mount Katahdin, Maine.* Oil on canvas. 30 x 40½". Edith and Milton Lowenthal Collection, Bequest of Edith Abrahamson Lowenthal, 1991. (1992.24.3) Photograph © 1992 The Metropolitan Museum of Art; **46** *Lighthouse at Two Lights.* Oil on canvas. 29½ x 43¼". Hugo Kastor Fund, 1962. (62.95) Photograph © 1990 The Metropolitan Museum of Art; THE MUSEUM OF MODERN ART, N.Y.: **81** *Christina's World.* Tempera on gessoed panel. 32¼ x 47¾". Purchase. Photograph © 1999 The Museum of Modern Art, New York; NATIONAL GALLERY OF ART, WASHINGTON, D.C.: **77b** *Right and Left.* Oil on canvas. 28¼ x 48⅜". Gift of the Avalon Foundation, © 1999 Board of Trustees, National Gallery of Art, Washington, D.C.; NATIONAL GEOGRAPHIC SOCIETY IMAGE COLLECTION: **12a** Maine flag. Illustration by Marilyn Dye Smith; **12b** Illustration by Robert Hynes; PHOTO RESEARCHERS: **14a** Photo by Andrew J. Martinez; PORTLAND MUSEUM OF ART, MAINE **18** *Wreck of the D. T. Sheridan.* Oil on canvas. 27⅜ x 43⅞". Bequest of Elizabeth B. Noyce, 1996.38.25. Photo Melville D. McLean; **63** *Group of Boats (Watching the Regatta).* Watercolor and graphite on paper. 11½ x 15¼". Bequest of Elizabeth B. Noyce, 1996.38.47. Photo Melville D. McLean; PRIVATE COLLECTION: **23** *Painting the Coast of Maine.* Oil on canvas. 14 x 14". Photo Peggy McKenna; PRIVATE COLLECTION **20** *Drift in Beach.* Oil on canvas. 30 x 72"; PRIVATE COLLECTION: **43** *Vinalhaven.* Oil on canvas. 60 x 60"; SCHMIDT BINGHAM GALLERY: **82** *Mount Kineo.* Casein on panel. 22 x 36"; *Matrix #8: Tide.* Silver prints with oil paint. 28⅝ x 35¾"; KEVIN SHIELDS: **89;** SPANIERMAN GALLERY: **57** *In a Kennebunkport Garden.* Oil on canvas. 24 x 30"